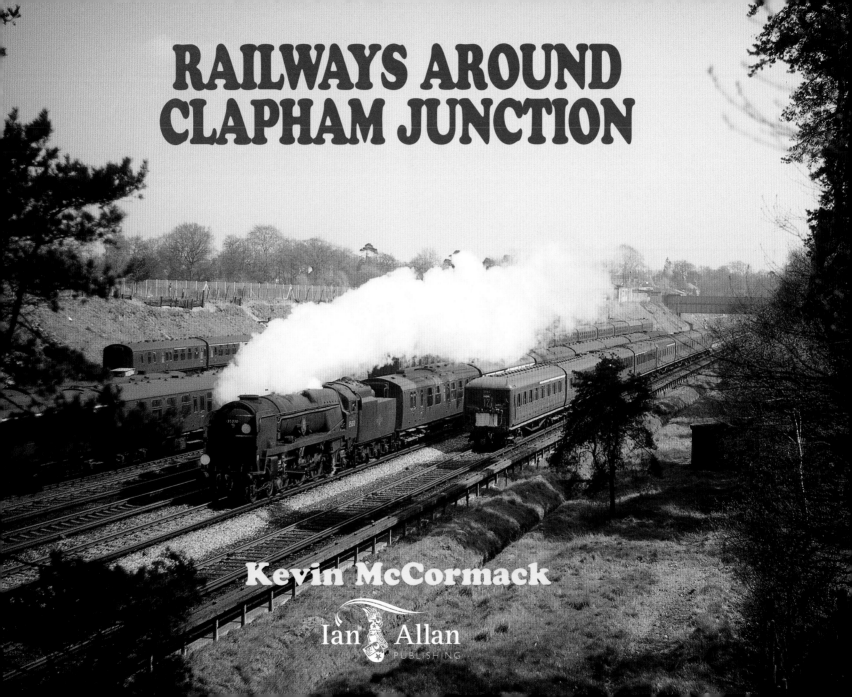

RAILWAYS AROUND CLAPHAM JUNCTION

Kevin McCormack

Ian Allan

PUBLISHING

Front cover: A Bournemouth train leaves Platform 9 at Waterloo in July 1964 hauled by 'West Country' Pacific No 34099 *Lynmouth*. Waterloo, even without the Eurostar terminal (which will be moving to St Pancras), is Britain's largest station. *Jim Oatway*

Back cover: 'King Arthur' No 30451 *Sir Lamorak* hauls the 2.54pm Waterloo–Basingstoke train through Walton-on-Thames in May 1960. The first series of 10 Maunsell 'Arthurs', of which No 30451 was the fourth, were built in 1925 as direct replacements for 10 Drummond 4-6-0s, whose tenders they originally took. *Jim Oatway*

Title page: In March 1967 rebuilt 'Merchant Navy' Pacific No 35030 *Elder Dempster Lines*, heading a down Bournemouth express, overtakes a '2-BIL' electric train between Walton-on-Thames and Weybridge, in a scene illustrating the bustle on lines serving Clapham Junction. *Vernon Murphy*

Left: This is Clapham Junction on 22 March 1967, showing the ancient, disused water tower at the western end of Platform 17. Standard Class 4 tank No 80154 has just brought in a train from Kensington Olympia. *Martin Jenkins / Online Transport Archive*

First published 2006

ISBN (10) 0 7110 3134 7
ISBN (13) 978 0 7110 3134 0

© Kevin McCormack 2006

Published by Ian Allan Publishing

an imprint of Ian Allan Publishing Ltd, Hersham, Surrey KT12 4RG
Printed in England by Ian Allan Printing Ltd, Hersham, Surrey KT12 4RG

Code: 0606/B1

Visit the Ian Allan Publishing website at www.ianallanpublishing.com

Introduction

Clapham, London, is famous for at least two things: the man on the omnibus who represents 'Joe Public' and the railway junction — the subject of this book — which proclaims itself to be Britain's busiest railway station. With some 2,000 train movements daily, it has also claimed to be Europe's busiest, having apparently seen off competition from Frankfurt.

Tragically, Clapham is also infamous: the cutting was the scene of a railway accident on 12 December 1988 which killed 35 people and left more than 100 injured when three trains collided as a result of a signalling defect.

Opened on 2 March 1863, Clapham Junction railway station was built as a joint venture between the London & South Western Railway (LSWR) and the London, Brighton & South Coast Railway (LBSCR), which companies, operating out of Waterloo and Victoria stations respectively, had decided to create an interchange station on the present site to replace their separate stations nearby (Clapham Common and New Wandsworth), as well as with the West London Extension Railway (WLER), in which each had a stake.

The railway had arrived in the Clapham area in 1838 with the opening of the first section of the London & Southampton Railway (renamed the following year as the LSWR). This initial 23-mile stretch from Nine Elms to Woking Common had six intermediate stations: Wandsworth (later called Clapham Common), situated in Clapham Cutting, Wimbledon, Kingston (now Surbiton), Ditton Marsh (now Esher), Walton-on-Thames and Weybridge. In 1848, following the construction of a 1¾-mile extension over nearly 200 railway arches, the London terminus moved from Nine Elms to Waterloo (called Waterloo Bridge until 1886). However, the LSWR originally wanted to get even closer to the City and actually constructed a line across the concourse at Waterloo station and over Waterloo Road (on the bridge which now carries pedestrians to Waterloo East) to link up with the South Eastern Railway and terminate at London Bridge station. However, this arrangement had limitations, and a better solution for reaching the City was eventually adopted by the LSWR — the building of the underground Waterloo & City line to the Bank.

The LBSCR had a more complicated history, acquiring various smaller undertakings during the 'railway mania' days of the mid-19th century, but suffice it to say that trains reached Wandsworth by 1856. Unlike the LSWR, the LBSCR already had access to the City (through having a terminus at London Bridge), but its objective now was to reach the lucrative, developing West End. However, due to the initial intransigence of the LSWR, the extension beyond New Wandsworth had to run alongside and then under this company's railway without connecting with it, in order to reach the initial terminus on the Thames embankment at Battersea Wharf (named Pimlico to make it sound more attractive to passengers) in 1858. Once Battersea Wharf had been reached, a railway bridge was then constructed over the River Thames (Victoria Bridge, later known as Grosvenor Bridge), and Victoria station constructed. Opened in 1860, the station was a joint venture with the London, Chatham & Dover Railway, whose trains came up from Beckenham and Herne Hill, thereby avoiding Clapham. The Great Western Railway also ran into Victoria via Addison Road station (later Kensington Olympia) following the opening of the WLER in 1863. The present Victoria station dates from 1908.

Fortunately for the travelling public, relations between the LSWR and LBSCR improved sufficiently for them to join up at Clapham Junction. The surrounding area was largely rural: lavender was grown there for the perfume industry (hence nearby Lavender Hill), and the Poupart family had extensive orchards (hence Poupart's Junction). The village of Clapham was more than a mile from the station site, which in fact is located in Battersea. However, Battersea was industrial and working-class, whereas Clapham was a fashionable village, so the railway companies, wishing to attract a more gentrified *clientèle*, named the station after Clapham. But at least Battersea can take comfort in having its name added to a power station (now disused, but likely to become a major leisure complex), as well as a famous dogs' home and a heliport! Furthermore, there is currently a campaign locally to rename the station 'Battersea Junction' or, failing that, 'Clapham Junction, Battersea', although it is hard to imagine this succeeding.

Architecturally, Clapham Junction station today is a fascinating hotch-potch of structures reflecting its diverse origins, and recent plans for its reconstruction have been shelved. The station is also a magnet for that increasingly rare human species associated with anoraks, vacuum flasks, notebooks and pencils — the trainspotter!

This 'Colour Portfolio', *Railways around Clapham Junction*, serves as a reminder of the trains which passed through the station in the final decade of Southern Region steam, which ended on 9 July 1967. All photographs are of working steam (or in a few cases electric units) at or within 20 miles of Clapham Junction. Grateful thanks go to the following contributors who have kindly loaned their colour transparencies (virtually all of which have never been seen in print before): Vernon Murphy, Nick Lera, Michael Allen, Colin Hogg, Jim Oatway, Geoff Rixon, Michael Furnell, Roy Hobbs, Neil Davenport, Harry Luff and Marcus Eavis. Thanks are also due to David Clark, for use of the late Ken Wightman's photographs, to Martin Jenkins, for the use of the Online Transport Archive material, and to Alan Sainty.

Kevin R. McCormack
Ashtead, Surrey
March 2006

Above: Steam was replaced on Waterloo–Exeter trains in May 1964, when the Western Region assumed responsibility for motive power. This view of Waterloo station on 14 June 1967 features 'Warship' diesel-hydraulic No D828 *Magnificent* (a possible overstatement!) and LMS-designed Ivatt Class 2 No 41319, which is shunting wagons. *Martin Jenkins / Online Transport Archive*

Right: 'West Country' Pacific No 34002 *Salisbury* is, literally, the centre of attention in this view of three types of motive power departing Waterloo station on 3 July 1966. Construction of the present station commenced in 1904, although it was 1922 before it was completed. The Windsor-line station (comprising Platforms 16-21) was built in 1885 and survived alongside the new building until demolished to make way for the Eurostar terminal. *Alan Sainty collection*

Left: A Royal Train normally travels along part of the Brighton line
at least once a year, carrying members of the Royal Family
from Victoria to Tattenham Corner for the Derby race meeting
on Epsom Downs. (They return by road.) Latterly, until 1962,
when the class was withdrawn, 'Schools' Class V locomotives
were used, and Stewarts Lane shed, which served Victoria station,
made a tremendous effort to impress. On the final 'Schools' working
No 30926 *Repton* (now preserved) passes Wandsworth Common
on 6 June 1962. *Roy Hobbs*

Above: Until displaced by Adams' larger 4-4-2 tanks (see page 38)
in the 1880s, Beattie 2-4-0 well tanks, built between 1863 and 1875,
provided the standard suburban motive power for Waterloo services.
By 1899 the entire class of 88 locomotives had been withdrawn,
except for three which were exiled to the Wenford Bridge mineral
line in North Cornwall. Following displacement in 1962, two
members of this trio (both now preserved) paid a final visit to their
old haunts and are seen on 2 December 1962 being prepared at Nine
Elms shed for a railtour. *Ken Wightman / David Clark collection*

Above: Hauling an up Bournemouth train composed (at least initially) of Bulleid carriages, 'Battle of Britain' No 34086 *219 Squadron* passes through Clapham Junction in the summer of 1965. A start appears to have been made on attempting to clean this locomotive. No fewer than 20 'West Country'/'Battle of Britain' Light Pacifics have been preserved, half of them in unrebuilt form with air-smoothed casing. *Vernon Murphy*

Right: From 1959, following electrification of the Kent main-line services, some steam locomotives were transferred to the South Western section. One such was ex-South Eastern & Chatham Railway (SECR) Class L 4-4-0 No 31768, dating from 1914, seen here heading a railtour through Surbiton station in September 1961. *Geoff Rixon*

Above: Urie-designed Class S15 express-freight 4-6-0 No 30506 hauls a van train through Walton-on-Thames in June 1962. Built by the LSWR in 1920 and distinguishable from the later Maunsell 'S15s' by its ribbed cab, this locomotive survives in preservation on the Mid-Hants Railway. *Nick Lera*

Right: Another LSWR Urie locomotive seen at Walton-on-Thames on the same day is No 30518, one of five Class H16 4-6-2 tanks built in 1921 for short-distance freight working from Feltham yard. These locomotives, together with the four 'G16' 4-8-0 tanks, were based initially at Strawberry Hill, until this became an electric-train depot following the construction of Feltham shed in 1923. *Nick Lera*

Above: Former LBSCR electric unit No 4510, operating a Shepperton service, leaves Clapham Junction in 1958. The LSWR began electric services in 1915, initially between Waterloo and Wimbledon via East Putney, but, unlike the LBSCR, used the third-rail system from the outset. The LBSCR had introduced electrification six years earlier, reaching Clapham Junction in 1911, but used overhead electric power. The Southern Railway converted the overhead to third rail between 1925 and 1928. Unit No 4510, which would survive until December 1959, was composed of stock built for the overhead system. *Marcus Eavis*

Right: Marsh Atlantic No 32425 *Trevose Head* heads a railtour from Victoria to Portsmouth through Epsom station on 3 May 1953. Eleven Atlantics of Classes H1 and H2 were built, but regrettably none was preserved. Following the surprise discovery of a suitable boiler, the Bluebell Railway in Sussex is in the process of constructing a new Atlantic. *Neil Davenport*

On the Oxted/East Grinstead line, a Lingfield race special, complete with Pullman car in the centre of the train, crosses Riddlesdown Quarry in December 1961 behind Class N Mogul No 31412. Designed by Maunsell while he was Chief Mechanical Engineer of the South Eastern & Chatham Railway, 80 of these locomotives were built between 1917 and 1934, No 31412 being the ante-penultimate.
Ken Wightman / David Clark collection

Further down the Oxted line, Standard Class 4 2-6-4T No 80081 climbs Woldingham Bank on 9 December 1961 with the 10.38am Victoria–Brighton service. Rather than taking the direct route to Brighton via Haywards Heath, the train will travel via Uckfield and Lewes, which line was not electrified.
Ken Wightman / David Clark collection

Above: Rebuilt 'Battle of Britain' Light Pacific No 34052 *Lord Dowding* (by now de-named but looking very smart nonetheless) pulls out from beneath the coaling stage at Nine Elms shed in May 1967. This engine was named after the Air Chief Marshal who was in charge of Fighter Command during the Battle of Britain (1940). *Nick Lera*

Right: A Victoria–Oxted train hauled by Standard Class 4 tank No 80088 comes off the flyover bringing the Brighton line over the South Western line near Pouparts Junction in May 1961. Central Division steam would be eliminated on 14 June 1965, but South Western steam would continue until 9 July 1967. *Jim Oatway*

Left: Maunsell 'King Arthur' No 30765 *Sir Gareth*, photographed from a passing train between Clapham Junction and Vauxhall, heads for Waterloo on 4 July 1959. Completed in May 1925, this locomotive would be withdrawn in September 1962. One example of this class, No 30777 *Sir Lamiel*, has been preserved.
Neil Davenport

Right and below right: Ivatt tanks were a familiar sight at Clapham Junction in the latter days of steam, as these two photographs taken six days before the end of Southern steam illustrate. No 41319 is climbing the bank behind 'B' 'box, bringing the 8.33am arrival from Kensington Olympia into Platform 17 before returning with the 8.46am. These were unadvertised services intended primarily for Post Office Savings Bank staff (before the office moved to Glasgow). A few minutes earlier No 41312 (since preserved) was photographed hauling empty stock from the carriage sidings past two young trainspotters and a very formidable station nameboard. This locomotive has recently been working freight trains on the Bluebell Railway, transporting soil from Imberhorne Tip, on the line's northern extension, to the Ardingly spur at Horsted Keynes.
Michael Furnell

Above: 'Schools' Class V 4-4-0 No 30935 *Sevenoaks* hauls a down Basingstoke train through Walton-on-Thames in May 1962. This class of 40 locomotives was the last new design of 4-4-0 in Great Britain (but not Ireland), and three — *Cheltenham*, *Repton* and *Stowe* — survive in preservation. They were ostensibly named after public schools, albeit with some latitude; for example, presumably due to limitations as to the size of nameplate the last member of the class, *Leatherhead*, was named after the location of the school rather than the institution itself, this being St John's, which has one of the nameplates on display. *Geoff Rixon*

Right: The Medway services were the last to be electrified before World War 2, such services being inaugurated in July 1939 using rakes of two-car sets known as '2-HAL' stock (with lavatories). Displaying an indecipherable stencil code on the front, unit No 2664 enters Vauxhall station on a down South Western service in May 1967. The clock tower housing Big Ben protrudes from the train's roof. *Nick Lera*

Having arrived on an inter-regional freight, BR Standard Class 4 2-6-0 No 76039, allocated to Kentish Town (London Midland Region) shunts at Clapham Yard on 16 April 1965. Above, looking as though it were designed to carry railway lines, is the enormously long and wide footbridge linking the platforms at Clapham Junction. In the distance, across the River Thames, is Fulham Power Station. *Geoff Rixon*

Storming past a 'Q1' Austerity locomotive in Wimbledon West goods yard is rebuilt 'West Country' No 34097 *Holsworthy*, heading the down 'Bournemouth Belle'. This prestigious and (latterly) extremely heavy Pullman train was introduced on 5 July 1931 and, prior to its temporary discontinuation caused by World War 2, was normally hauled by a 'Lord Nelson' 4-6-0 but occasionally by a 'King Arthur'. Following the train's reinstatement in 1946, the 'Merchant Navy' class provided the regular motive power, but, as seen here, Light Pacifics were also used. *Author's collection*

Left: Urie-designed Class S15 4-6-0 No 30503, built in 1920, emerges light-engine from the Addlestone line at Byfleet & New Haw (previously called West Weybridge) in May 1961. The class was originally intended for express-freight duties, but the locomotives proved sufficiently versatile to work passenger trains as well.
Jim Oatway

Above: A Drummond design for the LSWR which lasted into the 1960s was his '700'-class goods, dating from 1897 and totalling 30 locomotives. In creating this class Drummond was undoubtedly influenced by his design work for Scottish railway companies, because these locomotives were built in Glasgow and originally bore a close resemblance to the Caledonian Railway's 'Jumbo' 0-6-0s — until Urie ruined their appearance in 1921 by rebuilding them with larger boiler and extended smokebox. Against a fascinating Victorian backdrop, No 30346, viewed from West London Junction signalbox, hauls a coal train from Feltham to Nine Elms on 5 June 1961.
Jim Oatway

Left: Waterloo's distinctive signalbox, since demolished, came into use in 1936, replacing an overhead 'box which straddled the tracks. This view features rebuilt, de-named Bulleid Light Pacific No 34021 *Dartmoor* entering the station at the head of a morning commuter train from Basingstoke. *Vernon Murphy*

Above: Maunsell's Class N15 express passenger locomotives dating from 1925-7 were a development of Urie's earlier design from 1918-23. Following the decision in 1924 to bestow, on both types, names of — or associated with — the Knights of the Round Table, the class became known as 'King Arthurs'. This view, recorded during 1961 in the cutting between Berrylands and Surbiton, depicts No 30798 *Sir Hectimere* in charge of a down Basingstoke train. *Geoff Rixon*

Left: Rebuilt 'Battle of Britain' Pacific No 34089 *602 Squadron* takes the Brighton line past Emmanuel School, just west of Clapham Junction, with the 9.34am Ramblers' Association special from Victoria to Baynards on 29 July 1962. Construction of the Bulleid Light Pacifics began in 1945, the locomotives initially being intended for use on trains to/from the South West. However, some were also required for the South Eastern section, hence the decision to give these names associated with the 'Battle of Britain', which was fought largely in the skies above Kent. *Michael Allen*

Below left: '6-PUL' electric unit No 3043 takes the 1pm Victoria–Brighton service past Wandsworth Common on 3 April 1965. Twenty of these six-car main-line sets, each including a Pullman car, were introduced in 1932, and this particular set was one of three originally used for the 'City Limited' business train and classified '6-CIT'. *Michael Allen*

Right: The West London Railway from Kensal Green (London & North Western Railway) to Kensington and the WLER from Kensington to Clapham Junction provided a valuable north–south link across London. As a result the line came to be heavily used in the 1950s and '60s for inter-regional excursion trains, until this traffic was killed off by increased car ownership and the lure of cheap foreign holidays. On 27 July 1963 rebuilt 'West Country' No 34028 *Eddystone* hauls a northbound inter-regional excursion composed of Midland stock through Kensington Olympia. *Michael Allen*

Completed in 1950 and broken up in 1968, one of the last unrebuilt 'West Country' Pacifics to remain in service, No 34102 *Lapford* (here unnamed), hauls an early-morning commuter train from Basingstoke past Wimbledon 'C' signalbox. The line to Sutton diverges to the left. *Vernon Murphy*

The Southern Railway's final design for express electric stock resulted in the '4-COR' (four-coach corridor) units built in 1937/8 for the newly electrified Waterloo–Portsmouth services via Guildford and the Victoria–Portsmouth/Bognor Regis services via Dorking and Horsham. Unit No 3156, forming the rear portion of a 12-car formation, proceeds towards Clapham Junction on its way to Waterloo in September 1966. '4-COR' units were to run until September 1972, latterly on local services, and a complete set, unit No 3142, has since been preserved by the Southern Electric Group.
Nick Lera

'Battle of Britain' No 34057 *Biggin Hill* hauls a down Bournemouth train through Clapham Cutting in September 1966. Named after the famous wartime airfield which was home to Hurricane and Spitfire squadrons, this locomotive was a popular choice for railtours around this time, as evidenced by the silver paint. *Nick Lera*

Clapham Cutting again on the same day but closer to the Junction. Rebuilt 'Merchant Navy' No 35007 *Aberdeen Commonwealth*, with a down express, approaches St John's Hill bridge as a Routemaster bus heads for Hounslow on route 37. The 'Merchant Navy' class were the most powerful steam engines on the Southern but suffered a setback in 1953 when all were temporarily withdrawn after a driving-axle fracture was discovered. Cover was provided by Eastern Region Class V2 2-6-2s. *Nick Lera*

Drummond's highly successful 'M7' 0-4-4 tank engines were built between 1896 and 1911. Apart from one which was experimentally superheated and another which fell down the lift shaft serving the Waterloo & City line all lasted well into the 1950s, and some into the 1960s. A spotless No 30032 is seen shunting at Feltham shed on 13 May 1961. *Jim Oatway*

Viewed from West London Junction signalbox, which straddled the lines between Waterloo and Clapham Junction east of the carriage-washing plant, Class S15 No 30839, one of the later Maunsell machines, hauls empty carriage stock to Clapham Junction sidings on 15 October 1962.

The 'S15' mixed-traffic locomotives were, in effect, small-wheeled 'King Arthurs', and some remained in regular service until 1965. *Jim Oatway*

Left: A different perspective of Clapham Junction is provided by this view of 'Battle of Britain' Light Pacific No 34052 *Lord Dowding* taking the Brighton line on 5 June 1964, carrying members of the Royal Family to the Oaks (the 'fillies' Derby') at Epsom racecourse. *Michael Allen*

Below: On 30 January 1965 crowds lined railway embankments and back gardens to pay their last respects to Sir Winston Churchill as his body was carried by train from Waterloo to Hanborough (north of Oxford), via Reading, for burial at Bladon. Appropriately the funeral train, seen here near Barnes, was hauled by 'Battle of Britain' No 34051 *Winston Churchill* (since preserved), the hearse, a bogie van, being the second vehicle. The Western Region provided the mourners with more prosaic motive power for the return journey to Paddington in the form of 'Western' diesel-hydraulic No D1015 *Western Champion*. Rumour has it that Churchill had specifically requested that his funeral train depart from Waterloo, for the benefit of Général de Gaulle! *Author*

The 'T9' class of 66 4-4-0s was undoubtedly Dugald Drummond's most successful express type for the LSWR, several clocking up 60 years of service. No 120, built at Nine Elms Works in 1899, is preserved as part of the National Collection and in the early 1960s was kept in running order to work specials. It was also given some regular employment and at the time of this photograph (June 1962) was rostered to work the Saturdays-only 12.24pm Waterloo–Basingstoke train, seen here between Queenstown Road (Battersea) and Clapham Junction. *Jim Oatway*

As mentioned on page 7, the diminutive Beattie well tanks were replaced on LSWR suburban duties by the larger Adams 4-4-2 tanks, of which 71 were built between 1882 and 1885, most being taken out of use following electrification of these services from 1915. However, two were retained to cope with the sharp curves on the Axminster–Lyme Regis branch in Dorset, and a third, earlier sold out of service, was re-purchased in 1946 (and is now preserved on the Bluebell Railway as LSWR No 488). On 19 March 1961 one of the trio revisited its old haunts for a railtour and is seen at Waterloo's Platform 16. *Michael Allen*

Maunsell's mighty 'Lord Nelson' class of 16 locomotives, all named after famous sea lords, was designed to work 500-ton express trains at an average speed of 55mph. This view at Waterloo on 29 April 1961 depicts No 30856 *Lord St. Vincent* at the head of a railtour to Portsmouth Harbour. Turned out in November 1928, the locomotive would be withdrawn in September 1962. *Michael Allen*

Left: The 80-strong Standard Class 4MT 4-6-0s were designed at Brighton and built at Swindon. No 75069, constructed in 1955 (and now preserved on the Severn Valley Railway), leaves Sanderstead station with the 5.49pm Victoria–Groombridge train on 31 May 1962. *Colin Hogg*

Above: Two Light Pacifics, Nos 34102 *Lapford* and 34057 *Biggin Hill*, provide a stirring sight for fishermen on the River Thames as they cross Richmond Bridge at the head of a railtour to Dorset on 22 January 1967. The first railway bridge at this location was built in 1848 for the Richmond-line extension to Staines and Windsor; the replacement shown here was constructed in the years 1906-8 but is similar in appearance to the original. *Nick Lera*

With just a month of service remaining, Salisbury-based 'King Arthur' No 30451 *Sir Lamorak* hauls an up Salisbury train through Esher station in May 1962. By this time it had lost its original Drummond tender, which had been replaced by the bogie tender seen here. Behind is a Gresley wooden-bodied vehicle which has escaped from the Eastern Region. *Geoff Rixon*

'Lord Nelson' No 30861 *Lord Anson* speeds through Clapham Cutting with a down railtour on 2 September 1962. Arguably, the appearance of these fine looking locomotives was spoiled by the wide design of chimney necessitated by the fitting of a double blastpipe in later life. *Ken Wightman / David Clark collection*

Left: This view of Waterloo station from the signalbox features Class U 2-6-0 No 31804, a rebuild of a 'River' 2-6-4 tank. Twenty-one of these were built, but following the Sevenoaks disaster of 1927 all were converted to 2-6-0 tender engines in 1928, the rebuilds being distinguishable from other members of the 'U' class by the wheel-splashers on the running-plate. *Jim Oatway*

Above: Seen at the front of Feltham shed on 7 March 1962, in their last year of service, are 'Schools' 4-4-0 No 30934 *St Lawrence* and one of the four massive Class G16 4-8-0 tanks, No 30495, designed for gravity shunting at the nearby marshalling yards. The 'Schools' was lucky to survive World War 2: on the night of 10/11 May 1941 it received a direct hit from a bomb while standing on Cannon Street railway bridge with Class H tank No 1541, the pair having drawn a train clear of the platforms because the station roof was on fire. *Jim Oatway*

Left: 'West Country' Pacific No 34015 *Exmouth* catches the evening sunlight as it passes through Weybridge with the 5pm Waterloo–Salisbury semi-fast in September 1966. Withdrawal of unrebuilt Light Pacifics began in 1963, and the first rebuilds were withdrawn the following year, casting serious doubt over the economics of the rebuilding exercise. *Vernon Murphy*

Above: Steel-panelled '4-SUB' unit No 4696 has just left Clapham Junction as rebuilt 'Battle of Britain' Pacific No 34087 *145 Squadron* (by now nameless) approaches the station with an early-morning train from Bournemouth. This photograph of Clapham Cutting was taken from St John's Hill bridge; the Victoria–Brighton line can be seen diverging on the left. *Vernon Murphy*

Above: Because of their similarity to the ill-fated 'River' class, including the use of some parts from these locomotives, Maunsell's 'W' class were not employed on passenger duties. Frequently found on cross-region (transfer) freight trains, they were also used on empty-stock workings into and out of Waterloo. On 29 July 1962 No 31924 hauls the Pullman set for the 'Bournemouth Belle' out of Clapham Junction carriage sidings. *Michael Allen*

Right: 'Schools' No 30918 *Hurstpierpoint* brings a Manchester-bound inter-regional train along the Brighton line towards Clapham Junction on 7 August 1960. Built between 1930 and 1935, the 'Schools' were almost as powerful as the 'King Arthurs' but had the advantage of wider route availability and were particularly suited to the Hastings line, with its narrow tunnels. In this view the runner beans and cabbages (no doubt lovingly tended by railway staff in the days before the current 'scorched earth' policy of clearing embankments) seem to be thriving. *Colin Hogg*

A busy scene typifying the Clapham Junction approaches is created by two rakes of steel-bodied '4-SUB' non-corridor stock on suburban workings and 'Merchant Navy' No 35013 *Blue Funnel* hauling an up Waterloo express, which is about to pass beneath Trinity Road bridge. *Vernon Murphy*

Despite the loss of their nameplates during their last few months of service, clean Bulleid Pacifics at the head of named boat trains still created an impressive sight. Rebuilt and by now de-named

'West Country' No 34013 *Okehampton* heads south-west through Clapham Cutting, as seen from Freemasons Bridge. *Vernon Murphy*

Above: Britain's last Pacific tank to remain in service, Urie Class H16 No 30517 built in 1921, arrives at Chessington South on 2 December 1962 with the railtour initially hauled by the Beattie tanks (page 7). The Chessington branch, which left the Raynes Park to Epsom line at Motspur Park, was unusual in having been built as late as 1938/9. It would have been extended to Leatherhead had it not been for the outbreak of World War 2 and the introduction in 1947 of the 'green belt' legislation which prevented development immediately south of Chessington. Yet as recently as the early 1990s British Rail still owned a strip of land through Ashtead Woods, relinquishing it only when the City of London Corporation acquired what has now become a National Nature Reserve. *Geoff Rixon*

Right: One of many Southern 'escapees' from Barry scrapyard has been 'Battle of Britain' No 34067 *Tangmere*, seen here near Raynes Park at the head of the 2.56pm Waterloo–Basingstoke train on 5 June 1962. Named after the airfield (near Chichester) which was another home to Hurricane and Spitfire squadrons, this locomotive is fully restored to main-line running. *Nick Lera*

Above: Rebuilt, de-named 'West Country' Pacific No 34021 *Dartmoor* enters Clapham Junction with the 5pm Waterloo–Salisbury semi-fast in the spring of 1967. Of the 110 'West Country' and 'Battle of Britain' Light Pacifics constructed, no fewer than 60 were rebuilt. This work, carried out between 1957 and 1961, involved the provision of new valve-gear and the removal of streamlining. *Vernon Murphy*

Right: All 30 of the 'Merchant Navy' Pacifics, construction of which had commenced in 1941, were rebuilt between 1956 and 1959. This photograph depicts the 10.30am Waterloo–Bournemouth express, hauled by the last member of the class, No 35030 *Elder Dempster Lines* (now de-named), passing a '4-SUB' electric train entering Wimbledon Park sidings in the summer of 1967. By this time Durnsford Road power station (see page 70) had been demolished (in 1965) to make way for the construction of East Wimbledon electric-train depot, which would open in 1974. *Vernon Murphy*

Above: Eastleigh-based 'West Country' No 34033 *Chard* hauls a Bournemouth–Waterloo train past Esher golf course on 12 March 1965, its last year of service. Turned out by Brighton Works in July 1946, this locomotive would be broken up barely 20 years later. *Geoff Rixon*

Right: 'M7' 0-4-4 tank No 30053, built at Nine Elms Works in 1905 and officially withdrawn in May 1964, approaches Shepperton at the head of a railtour on 5 July 1964! Subsequently purchased by an American museum and shipped to Vermont, the locomotive has now returned to this country and can be found on the Swanage Railway. *Roy Hobbs*

Above left: Despite considerable opposition the celebrated 'Brighton Belle', the world's first all-Pullman electric train, was withdrawn on 30 April 1972, having run since 1933, when the Brighton line was electrified. By the end the trio of five-car sets had been disfigured by being painted blue and grey, but this shot near Coulsdon in September 1966 shows the 'Belle', with unit No 3052 nearest the camera, in all its glory, just before the Pullman crest was blotted out by a high-visibility yellow panel. *Nick Lera*

Left: In 1941 the Southern Railway built two Co-Co electric locomotives, designed by Rowath (Chief Electrical Engineer) and Bulleid (Chief Mechanical Engineer), which became Nos 20001 and 20002. A third locomotive, No 20003, appeared in 1948

with detail differences, the main external one being the absence of the sloping roofline at the front. It is seen here near Coulsdon on a Victoria–Newhaven boat train, also in September 1966. *Nick Lera*

Above: Although the 'Bournemouth Belle' Pullman train was converted from steam to diesel traction in January 1967, occasional substitutions by steam still occurred until the train's demise on 9 July. De-named 'West Country' No 34023 *Blackmore Vale* (now preserved on the Bluebell Railway) heads the up 'Belle' through Clapham Junction on 15 June, an apparently contrived diesel failure having allowed the unrebuilt Pacific a final fling on this prestigious working. *Vernon Murphy*

Left: Introduced in 1889, the Adams 'O2' 0-4-4 tanks were best known for being the mainstay of Isle of Wight passenger services from the 1920s to the 1960s, the island examples being fitted with enlarged bunkers and Westinghouse brakes. One of those which remained on the mainland was No 30199, built at Nine Elms Works in 1891 and pictured here on 25 March 1962 hauling a three-coach enthusiasts' special over the Shepperton branch. Behind Fulwell station house can be seen the famous tram/trolleybus depot, now a bus garage. *Michael Allen*

Above: A spotless 'Merchant Navy' Pacific at the head of the down 'Bournemouth Belle' meets an equally clean Mogul hauling an engineering train at Raynes Park in March 1962. Someone in the first carriage of the latter train is peering out, probably having noticed that the door of the van has been left open. *Colin Hogg*

Left: Rebuilt 'Battle of Britain' No 34089 *602 Squadron* leaves Platform 17 at Clapham Junction with an excursion to Brighton from the Western Region on 2 September 1962. Behind the cab of the locomotive is the water tower featured on page 2. In the background, above the retaining wall, is the former LBSCR station building at St John's Hill, dating from 1910 and now restored. *Michael Allen*

Above: Nameplates and cleanliness did not always go together in the latter days of Southern Region steam. Indeed, pictures of Bulleid

Pacifics with nameplates intact but in disgraceful external condition have been largely omitted from this book in favour of de-named clean examples, illustrating the special effort made at many sheds to return them to respectability for their final months of service. Bucking the trend, by carrying nameplates *and* being surprisingly clean in the final winter of Southern steam, rebuilt 'West Country' No 34013 *Okehampton* speeds through Esher in December 1966 on a down Bournemouth express. *Author*

Left: 'Battle of Britain' Light Pacific No 34054 *Lord Beaverbrook* stands on the turntable at Nine Elms shed in June 1961. The site would be cleared after closure of the shed in July 1967 and is now home to Covent Garden fruit and vegetable market. Lord Beaverbrook, the newspaper magnate, was Minister of Aircraft Production at the time of the Battle of Britain. *Ken Wightman / David Clark collection*

Above: Two Dugald Drummond locomotives stand at East Croydon station on 15 September 1963 at the head of a railtour from Victoria to the Bluebell Railway. Class T9 4-4-0 No 120, dating from 1899, is back on that railway today, while Caledonian single No 123, built in 1886, is in the Glasgow Transport Museum. Drummond had been Locomotive Superintendent on the Caledonian Railway (and the North British) before moving to the LSWR. *Geoff Rixon*

65

Above: This grassy and rarely photographed spot on the northern side of the South Western main line east of Clapham Junction (close to the carriage-washing plant) provides the setting for 'U'-class 2-6-0 No 31621 hauling a freight bound for Stewarts Lane. *Jim Oatway*

Right: Waiting at Victoria station is the stand-by Royal Train locomotive for the 1959 Epsom Derby race meeting, 'Schools' 4-4-0

No 30915 *Brighton*, beautifully turned out by Stewarts Lane shed. Following electrification of the Brighton line in 1933 most of the steam locomotives latterly based at this shed worked Kent-line passenger trains which did not pass through Clapham Junction, these services not being electrified until 1959 and 1961. The tank engines used for suburban services from Victoria were normally based at the other end of the lines on which they worked. *Michael Allen*

Left: British Rail corporate colours are beginning to oust the familiar Southern green livery in this view of de-named 'West Country' Pacific No 34025 *Whimple* hauling a down Bournemouth train through Wimbledon. The platform on the left (since demolished) was built in 1892 for the Wimbledon Common reviews and was also used for troop trains during World War 1; latterly it was used for parcels traffic. *Vernon Murphy*

Above: The LSWR reached Windsor in 1849 and built its station at the foot of the Castle, beside the River Thames, complete with Royal waiting room. In this picture taken on 30 April 1966 Standard Class 5MT 4-6-0 No 73114 *Etarre*, its name taken from a withdrawn 'King Arthur', approaches Windsor & Eton Riverside on a railtour. *Vernon Murphy*

Above: Introduced in 1914, the 'H15s' were Urie's first 4-6-0s, and the class of 26 comprised a mixture of new engines (including some later Maunsell locomotives) and Urie rebuilds of unsuccessful Drummond 4-6-0s. One of the new Urie engines, No 30486, is seen passing Durnsford Road power station (see page 55 for comparison shot) on 30 August 1958 with the 11.56am Waterloo–Salisbury train. The power station, opened in 1913 to provide current for the third-rail electrification, closed down in 1958 after the Southern Region switched to obtaining its electricity supply from the National Grid. *Colin Hogg*

Right: Salisbury-based rebuilt 'Battle of Britain' Pacific No 34056 *Croydon* approaches Esher (for Sandown Park) station at the head of a down express. Although best known as a civil aerodrome, Croydon was also a Battle of Britain station, as was nearby Kenley. *Geoff Rixon*

Left: Viewed from the LT District Line station at West Brompton, Standard Class 3 2-6-2 tank No 82019 hauls a Kensington Olympia– Clapham Junction train past the site of the WLER station in early July 1967, immediately prior to dieselisation. This was the last steam-hauled suburban service in London. Behind the LT station can be seen Earl's Court Exhibition Hall. *Harry Luff*

Above: With Maunsell coach and goods van in tow, Bulleid Austerity 'Q1' 0-6-0 No 33003 heads for Clapham Junction sidings on 29 July 1962. Built in 1912, the elevated signalbox (known as 'A' 'box) would partially collapse in May 1965, wreaking havoc with services. *Michael Allen*

An Oxted-line train from Victoria approaches Clapham Junction in 1958 hauled by Standard Class 4 2-6-4 tank No 80018. The building on the right (with the tall cupola) is the Arding & Hobbs department store dating from 1910, which replaced the first shop opened in 1885 and destroyed by fire in 1909. This famous landmark is now owned by Debenhams. *Ken Wightman / David Clark collection*

Before the arrival of the Standard Class 4 tanks on the Southern in the late 1950s, Victoria commuter trains on non-electrified lines were in the hands of LMS-designed Fairburn tanks introduced in 1945, which in turn had replaced earlier LBSCR types. On 14 June 1959 Brighton-built No 42087 hauls the 9.8am to Tunbridge Wells West out of Victoria and up Grosvenor Bank. Two Fairburn tanks (Nos 42073 and 42085) survive in preservation. *Colin Hogg*

Above: One of the few LBSCR types still to be seen in the area covered by this book during the late 1950s/early 1960s was Billinton's 'E4' class of 0-4-4 tanks, designed for secondary passenger and mixed-traffic duties. No 32472, photographed while shunting at Clapham Junction in May 1962, was built at Brighton in 1898. Sister No 32473 (better known as *Birch Grove*) is happily preserved on the Bluebell Railway. *Roy Hobbs*

Right: In the days before Bulleid Pacific domination on the South Western following electrification of the Kent lines, 'Lord Nelson' No 30865 *Sir John Hawkins*, dating from 1929, heads the 11.30am Waterloo–Weymouth express through Wimbledon on 20 August 1960. The last of its class to be built, this locomotive would be the first withdrawn, in May 1961. The original engine, No 30850 *Lord Nelson*, has been preserved. *Colin Hogg*

Left: Rebuilt, de-named 'West Country' No 34018 *Axminster* approaches Vauxhall with an up Southampton boat train in early 1967. Despite increasing airline domination there was still considerable liner traffic at this time, with connecting boat trains provided, many of which carried special headboards. *Vernon Murphy*

Above: Maunsell had a hand in the design of the long-lived '2-BIL' electric units, which were introduced in 1937 and were to last into the early 1970s. This view looking west features unit No 2108 at Weybridge station in the summer of 1966. The line diverging on the right goes to Addlestone, Chertsey and Virginia Water. *Vernon Murphy*

Built in 1942, the 40 members of Bulleid's powerful 'Q1' class were designed to incorporate the largest boiler and firebox possible on an 0-6-0, with the minimum of frills. In June 1965 an unusually clean

No 33006 is turned at Nine Elms shed, the driver or fireman being seen working the wheel on the extreme left. *Nick Lera*